GRAN GRAN'S ANGEL

About the Author

Living on the outskirts of a friendly village, surrounded by fields and trees, with a view of the river Medway, I am at peace. I haven't always lived here, in fact this is the first time I have lived alone in all my fifty-something years, with my faithful companion Bride, my golden retriever.

I don't consider myself qualified to be called an author, but once again, I have been guided to take a leap of faith and here I am having my work published. I am an avid reader, I like to lose myself and live another life through the books I read. I enjoy anything that can transport me to another place, to see the sights and smell the smells.

What can I say about myself, other than that I am an ordinary gel who has had some extraordinary experiences. I love people and hearing their stories – life after all is a story, and we all have a story to tell. After the struggles and sorrows I've had, I am truly blessed to be where I am now and I hope that by reading this book you will be blessed too.

Gran Gran's Angel

Leigh Norris

SilverWood

Published in paperback 2012 by SilverWood Books, Bristol, BS1 4HJ
www.silverwoodbooks.co.uk

ISBN 978-1-78132-049-5

British Library Cataloguing in Publication Data
A CIP catalogue record for this book is available from the British Library

Set in Goudy by SilverWood Books
Printed on responsibly sourced paper

With Thanks

I dedicate this book firstly to the glory of God, without whom it wouldn't have been written.

For my Nan, Edith Mary Axon, who is at its heart. For my children, Zoe and Chris, who have stood beside me through the good times and the not so good. Thank you for always believing in me. And finally for my Grandson Harry, the joy of my life and a gift from God when I needed him the most. "Who loves you all the world Harry? Grandma does."

I also have to thank all those who answered my prayer for help in raising the money to get this published: Zoe, Malc and Harry, Chris, Mum, Janice, Don, Ian and Marje, Christine, Sylvia, Glyn and Bryony, Ann, Sue, Paul, Peter and Doreen, Graham, Ian and Sarah, The Women's Fellowship and the Friends of the Community. Thank you and may God bless you all mightily.

Leigh

To my Nan
For all your support and guidance

Contents

List of Images

Gran Gran's Angel

I was woken by the big guns firing, so I got out of bed and went to look out of the window, and there, hanging in the sky, caught in the cross-beams of the searchlights, was an angel. I rubbed my eyes, pinched myself and said out loud, "Can it be true?"

I looked again. It was still there, its head bowed and its wing hanging down. It was so clear, I could count the feathers and they were the colour of mother-of-pearl.

This book has been a long time in coming to be written, because I always thought that when I came to write it, it would be about my Nan, her life and her faith. What I have come to learn is that my life and hers are so closely interwoven, and as all things are done in God's time, only now is it right to attempt what He is guiding me to do.

What you have just read is my Nan's description of what she saw from her attic bedroom, during the First World War. She was in service to a family at the time. The following morning, she told the children's nurse what she had seen, only to be "poo-pooed" by her. Nan never told me what the nurse's reaction was, when later in the week, there was a report in the newspaper, describing how a Dr Flood had seen the same thing!

My story starts here because I grew up hearing that description and never tired of hearing it. I was always asking about "the angel". I spent a lot of time with Nan and my bedtime stories were Bible stories. I didn't think about it at the time but, in retrospect, I realise that she never read the stories. She knew them all by heart. At three years old my usual request was for, "How they found the baby Jesus". The story came to life for me. I could see the rich clothing that the kings wore. I could smell the sheep and goats that the shepherds were guarding. I could feel the heat of the fire as they sat on the ground, and of course the appearance of the angel was just as it should be. So you see, for me, Jesus was part of my family.

Oh, by the way, the angel became known as "Gran Gran's" because that was the name my children called her and it stuck.

Me in Nan and Grandad's garden at age four

Early Memories

Mum, Dad and I lived with my maternal grandparents until I was about four years old. We then moved to our own home, although I was always with Nan and Grandad when Mum and Dad were at work. I loved being with them. They always had time for me. I can remember sitting on my Grandad's lap at the dining table, with its red chenille tablecloth, reading to him from the newspaper. I was three years old. There was a calm and warmth in their home, what with the open fire in the front room and the smell of the copper boiler on wash day. There was always the smell of baking. Nan's jam and treacle tarts were something to behold.

Without realising it they shaped my thinking, and their morals and beliefs became my backbone. They never shouted or smacked me. I never heard them say a cross word to each other or to anyone else, for that matter. Grandad was retired but he always had some "project" on the go, be it painting or tending his small allotment at the bottom of the garden. He grew prize roses, and I thought it a great treat to be allowed to use the stirrup pump to water them with feed. Nan worked hard in the home. She did all the laundry by hand, the "whites" boiled to within an inch of their lives in the old copper boiler that had to be lit underneath to heat the water. A "blue dolly bag" was added to help the whites look whiter! I can remember being allowed to turn the handle of the mangle when she wrung out the sheets. I seem to recall there was a lot of steam and her glasses were constantly being wiped on her apron. The sheets pegged onto the line and flapping away in the breeze always made me feel safe somehow.

When I was five Mum bought me a pram, baby doll and knitted a complete wardrobe of clothes for my Christmas present. She was going to have a baby the following February, and we were going to push our prams together. Unfortunately, her blood pressure rocketed and she spent weeks in hospital on bed rest. I wasn't worried, though. I was staying with Nan and Grandad and attending their local school. Although I did walk out one play time and went home, as I didn't like having to learn the times table "parrot fashion", we didn't do that in my school!

Dad used to take me into town on Saturday afternoons so that I could wave to Mum at the window of the hospital. I quite enjoyed the trip because we would always go into Woolworth's afterwards, where I would scramble onto one of the shiny stools to drink my banana milkshake. Happy were the days when I felt loved and secure. Everything was right with my world and the new baby was going to make it perfect.

to DEAR MUMMY: I HAVE
SHREDDED. WHEN I EVERY DAY
FOR MY BREAKFAST. AND I EAT ALL
MY DINNER UP. I HOPE YOU
DO THE SAME.
    I HAVE ONE SHILLING
  AND SEVENPENCE WHICH I
AM SAVING FOR THE
BABY.
  I HOPE ARE FEELING
BETTER AND WILL BE HOME
BECAUSE I LOVE YOU.
      LOTS OF LOVE
      FROM
        ELAINE
x x x x x x x x x + + + + + r + + x x f x f x f x x x x x

The letter I sent to my mum when she was in hospital expecting
the baby, written at age five. (Elaine is my Christian name, but I've
been called Leigh since I was young.)

Me with Nan and Grandad at Southend

Nan and Grandad

Tragedy Strikes

14 February 1963, Valentine's Day – the day I saw my dad cry for the first time. He sat me on his lap to tell me that the baby, a little boy, wouldn't be coming home because he had gone to Jesus.

I would be six in two months time and was to be a "big" girl and help Mummy when she came home. Little did I know at that tender age that my life would never be the same again. I was happy to have my mum back, but it wasn't the same mum who had left me to go into hospital. This mum played Jim Reeves records over and over, and knelt on the floor with her head in the armchair, sobbing, hardly noticing I was there.

We were back in our own home, Dad was at work and I was taking myself to and from school. I was confused as to why Mum was upset. Wasn't the baby, Vincent, with Jesus? Why should she be in such a state if my brother was safe in Heaven? Mum gave away her pram and all the clothes she had knitted. My pram and baby doll? I never played with them.

I don't know when the Sunday night ritual of raised voices and arguments started. All I know is I would be woken by the noise from the lounge, below my bedroom, and would stand at the top of the stairs crying and begging them to stop. I was afraid to call out too loudly, afraid to go down, and even more afraid when the shouting stopped because I didn't know what was happening. I would go back to bed and cry myself to sleep, not understanding what I had done to cause my parents' unhappiness. I had tried to be "big" and to be good but it must be my fault... Mum once said to me, "Of course your dad wanted a boy, but he's got you." To my young ears that sounded like I wasn't good enough. I wasn't what my dad really wanted.

In retrospect, perhaps she meant that he should be grateful for what he had – me. But what I heard and carried inside me would last for many years, just underneath the surface, *You're not good enough.*

From this time until I was nine, my life settled into a routine. I went home for lunch after having tried school dinners and being forced to eat carrots (which I told the dinner lady I didn't like, and was promptly sick all over her shoes). Unfortunately, Mum was rarely in when I arrived home, so I would climb in the kitchen window and hope that she would get in with something to eat before I had to go back to school. When I was lucky, she would arrive with a saveloy and chips, which I would eat whilst hurrying back to school. On not so lucky days, I would go back to school with an empty stomach!

I would see Nan and Grandad on Saturdays when I would enjoy cuddles and goodies to eat. Why didn't I tell

Nan what was going on at home? I couldn't; that would have been disloyal and what if she decided it was my fault? I couldn't risk Nan changing too, and anyway I had told Jesus what was happening and how I felt. I said my prayers every night and asked him to help Mummy and Daddy, and to let them love me again.

I made some friends at school, the ones on the fringes. The "fat" girl who no one wanted to play with and the girl who was one of six children who smelt of wee. I didn't hanker after being one of the "popular" girls. They always seemed a bit spiteful to me. I was much happier with those whom Jesus would have befriended.

Me and teddy with Nan and Grandad in their garden at age four

My First Experience of Loss

Although my brother had been stillborn, I can't say I felt I had lost him. So, although I had experienced a bereavement, I didn't class it as that.

When I was nine, my Grandad was ill and in hospital. I was taken to visit him but had to be sneaked in, as children weren't allowed on the ward. Praise the Lord that things have improved and the health service is more enlightened. That was the last time I saw him. He died in hospital. I didn't understand why God had taken him from me.

I was very angry with God and wasted no time in telling Him so. How could He do this to me? Wasn't I going through enough without losing my dearest Grandad? I might have been only nine, but I had to grow up fast, to survive; and I now had my first taste of feeling alone.

Throughout all the disturbing times since I was five, I had always had Jesus to turn to, to talk to, and I absolutely believed He heard me and loved me. Now, I was too angry to talk to Him anymore. What was the point? He let my

Grandad die… my Grandad who I missed and wanted back.

Isn't it amazing how God works? There I was, feeling sorry for myself when really I should have known that God had it all in hand. My Nan went down with shingles and was very ill. It was too difficult for my Mum to nurse her in her own home, so Nan moved in with us. Result!

Okay, so I got to spend more time with Nan. Having her around and grieving for Grandad with her allowed me to talk to God again. I went back to Sunday School, after having turned my back on Church too. I started to feel close to Him again. Having Nan around helped my fear to subside. I had always felt afraid – a horrible sick feeling deep inside. If asked, I couldn't have told anyone what I was afraid of. I still can't hear about anyone living in fear without praying for them and wanting to help. Fear, for me, is one of the most soul-destroying things.

Nan recovered and I found life a lot easier with her around. She took over the cooking, so at least now I got a hot meal every day. During this time, I had a friend called Paul. He was an only child, like me. His parents were older and a bit old-fashioned. I think he liked me because I was fun and a bit daring. If there was a tree to climb, I'd be the first one up it. We spent the summer holidays together, making camps and using our *I Spy* books to identify different trees, birds and leaves. We made up clubs that had a list of rules and secret passwords. We had a clubhouse in his dad's shed where we ate our sandwiches and drank our lemonade. I would go indoors at the end of the day feeling tired, happy and looking forward to the next day. Great times.

Me and Grandad in his garden at age six

I can't remember why now, but Paul wasn't around for a couple of days, so I played with some other friends. I came home one day as Paul's mum was leaving our house, and she looked like she had been crying. My Mum said she had something to tell me: Paul had died. It turned out that he had been crawling after a lizard through a pipe, fell out of the end and drowned in a pool of water. They weren't so hot on Health & Safety back then. I missed Paul but again, I had that sense that he was safe with Jesus. I spent a lot of time with Paul's mum and she seemed to take comfort from me talking about Paul and what we used to get up to.

She and her husband moved away, but I did hear that they had another baby, a little girl. A blessing from God. They called her Grace.

Around the same time, another friend was killed. She was hit by a car whilst crossing a road. She was with another girl, and while I didn't know her at the time, the girl that wasn't hit would turn out to be the cousin of my future husband!

Hit by Illness

I was lying on the sofa on a Saturday afternoon, watching the wrestling on the TV. Mum was saying something to me. I could see her mouth moving but her words didn't make any sense. What? *What is she saying?* It was all going over my head…

This was the start of an illness that took time to diagnose and from which I almost died. I remember my Dad carrying me into the hospital. I was in my pyjamas and wrapped in a tartan travelling blanket. The previous few months I had been either in bed or on the sofa. My weight plummeted. I couldn't eat. My skin fell off. My hair, nails and eyelashes fell out. The light hurt my eyes. I was too weak to stand.

However, the day I'll describe was the day I got to see the specialist. He was going to tell us what was wrong with me. I remember him well – a very tall, red-bearded Scotsman. He asked for me to undress. Having examined my naked little body, he said to my dad, "Do you know what this is?"

My Dad in his frustration said, "No, I wouldn't be here if I did."

"Drug poisoning," came the diagnosis. "What has this child taken?"

A debate ensued and then Mum told him about the "worm medicine" she had given me. The specialist got on the phone to the pharmacist where Mum had bought the *jollop* to find out what ingredients it had in it. He decided on what had caused me to be so ill and prescribed an ointment that was to be applied twice a day all over my body.

Gradually, I improved and no longer left a trail of "me" when I moved. Throughout the illness, I didn't fear death. In fact, there were times when I welcomed the thought of going to Jesus. I saw Jesus a couple of times. I didn't tell anyone because I thought they would put it down to my being so poorly. I did see Him though, just smiling at me and letting me know I would get well.

I lost a lot of schooling during this time but, when I was well enough, I devoured every book I could get my hands on. I have always loved reading and have taught myself a lot. I managed to get back to school and started at a Church of England senior school. I got involved with the Scripture Union and sang in the choir. Religious Education was my favourite subject and I was forever asking questions of my teacher. I had a burning desire to learn as much as I could about Jesus and His ministry. It was then that I started to read the Bible earnestly. Every Tuesday, I would walk to meet Mum and Nan from the Derby & Joan club that they went to.

For a couple of weeks around that time, I had complained about my legs aching. Mum put it down to "growing pains", as I'd had a growth spurt. Then came the morning when Mum called me to get up for school. I went to swing my legs out of bed and nothing happened! I was paralysed from the waist down. The doctor was called and for the next two weeks he visited every day, sometimes twice a day, even at the weekend. I remember one day he arrived with these huge books which he plonked on the floor as he sat on my bed going through them. He thought at first that I might have polio. He continually checked my heart while reassuring me I would soon be A1.

Following a lot of tests, I was diagnosed with Rheumatic Fever. The medication I was on kept the fever at bay and thankfully my heart was not affected. It was during this illness that I came to know Jesus as my saviour and I gave my life to Him.

I spent many months in bed. Jesus was my constant companion. I spoke to Him every day. It was during one of these times that He revealed to me that I was special and that He had work for me to do. I was aware of His peace and didn't doubt that I would walk again and be well.

My education was suffering again, so I was supplied with a home tutor for a few hours a week. Following a year in a wheelchair and physiotherapy, I did indeed walk again, and walked taller, as I had had another growth spurt.

Little did I know then, God would use this experience later in my life.

Someone of My Own

Mum was an entertainer – a talented pianist and comedienne. She played in a band, and most Friday and Saturday evenings she was out on a booking. She also played at a local working men's club and Dad would be in the men's bar playing snooker. It was whilst I was sitting in the hall one Saturday evening that I first set eyes on the young man who was to become my husband.

He had popped in for a quick drink with a friend as it was his eighteenth birthday. I was sitting with someone he knew and we were introduced. Within days we were dating. I was three months short of my fourteenth birthday. I fell in love. Totally. I had someone all of my own and it seemed that God had sent him to me. Although our families didn't know each other, his mum had knitted a matinee jacket for his grandmother to give to my mum to give to me. Phew! You see, his nan went to a Derby and Joan club where my mum sometimes played the piano. And to top it all, there is a card in my baby book from his nan.

So you can see why I thought he had been sent to me... can't you?

Anyway, sent or not we embarked on a courtship and married when I was sixteen. We bought a house, had three children and settled down to married life. Like any young couple, we experienced happy times, tough times and some downright scary times. Money was tight, as I stayed at home to raise our children until the youngest went to school. Then I worked in school kitchens so that I was at home during the holidays. If I'm honest, God took a back seat during this time. I was too busy *living*. If only I had sought Him out earlier, things might have turned out differently.

My husband had anger issues, was violent and jealous. This had all started when we were courting, but hey, I was young, in love and he would change! I don't want to dwell on it, as I have forgiven him – to set myself free, *not* to condone his behaviour. As you can imagine, it put a huge strain on our relationship.

To backtrack a little, my dad had been taken ill the year before I married. He was diagnosed with emphysema and, five years later, cancer. It was hard trying to get to London to visit him in hospital, as I didn't drive then. When he came home he spent nearly every day with me. He would turn up, have a cup of tea while my younger ones played and we would talk for hours. He had always said he was an atheist, but now we were talking about God and faith. I remember him asking me what I believed in and why. That day flew by!

When he was taken into hospital locally, he asked

me to speak to his consultant about his condition and prognosis. Having been the one to tell him he had cancer in the first place, he had asked me to tell him the truth, so I did. I know he trusted me to ask the questions he wanted answered and to tell him. So an appointment was made, and one Sunday afternoon I met with the consultant's intern. He was only a young man and obviously nervous, but I had to ask the painful questions for my dad.

I had prayed before going into this meeting, as I had started praying again when Dad was first diagnosed. I must admit, I felt guilty about praying as I knew in my heart that I wasn't honouring Him as I should. I was "using" Him because I wanted something.

Anyway, back to the meeting…

I asked this poor young chap, "Is my dad dying?"

After a long pause, where his shoes suddenly became the most fascinating thing to look at, he replied, very quietly, "Yes, now, he is."

I thanked him for being straight with me and then told him that it was Dad's request not to be resuscitated. He agreed that it would be written in the notes.

You may be wondering where my mum was at this time. She was there, with a face like thunder. I'm sure she felt I was usurping her position as Dad's wife, but he had asked me to do this as he knew she couldn't. When I told Dad the outcome of the meeting, he was quiet for a while. Then he carried on talking about everyday things, like what the children had been up too.

The next time I visited he asked me to do him one last favour. I agreed, and then he asked me to go to a certain undertaker, whom he knew, and arrange his funeral. With a bit of trepidation, I phoned for an appointment and promptly did just that. I reported back to Dad and gave him the quote for the cost. During the last two weeks of his life, he drifted in and out of sleep. I saw him on the Sunday and he hardly knew I was there. The following Tuesday, God intervened and gave me such a huge blessing that I still thank him today, some thirty-one years later.

This is how it happened...

My in-laws were visiting with me for the day. My husband was on a 2–10 shift at work. Just before 5:30, my husband phoned to say that he could leave work if I wanted to go and see Dad. Of course I jumped at the chance. The children were taken care of, as my in-laws would baby-sit. Just after 6 pm, I walked into my dad's room.

He was sitting up in bed and was really surprised to see us, but not as surprised as I was to see him sitting up and awake! He said he fancied a really cold glass of milk and, as he hadn't been eating or drinking, I was only too pleased to get him one. He downed it in one and then asked for another!

We sat and talked, and he asked me to collect an envelope and take it to his bank manager. I said I would. Then we talked about personal stuff and, for the first time in all those months, I broke down and cried in front of him. I grabbed his hand and said I didn't want to lose him and that I didn't want him to be angry with me. I can still hear the words he spoke today: "I love you too much to be angry with you."

I was twenty-three-years old, he was fifty-six and that

was the one and only time that he told me he loved me. It was worth the wait.

Upon leaving, I collected the envelope and we went home. The children were in bed and I can see myself now, kneeling on my living room floor, saying to my in-laws, "If he goes tonight, I'm happy to let him go."

In the early hours of the following morning, Mum rang to say we needed to get to the hospital. We took the children to my in-laws and as I rang the doorbell of my mum's house, she had just come off the phone. Dad had gone, as I knew he would. He had told me the night before that he didn't want us sitting around his bed, watching him die. More importantly, he had told me he knew Jesus.

Oh, you're wondering about the envelope? It contained his will and a cheque for the cost of his funeral.

Life Goes On

My twenties and thirties saw me involved in my children's lives. Cubs, Brownies, football and judo to name a few of the activities they were involved in. I worked my way up in the school kitchens to become Assistant Cook. My husband had gone into business with friends and when one of them pulled out, he took it over. There were always problems with people paying on time, if at all…

Money was getting to be a real problem – the lack of it, that is. So I took in knitting for a firm. I had two weeks to make an Angora wool "picture" jumper that were all the rage in the 80s. It was a horrible job as the wool got up my nose and there were so many ends to sew in. I would sit up all night sometimes just to get them finished.

When I passed my driving test at thirty, I was able to get a job in the bakery at a shopping centre during the evenings. So, I was juggling my family commitments and holding down three jobs. My Mum and I had become estranged and she had moved, with Nan, to another town.

My husband's jealous outbursts continued and, as the children were now older and more aware, I worried about what they saw and heard.

I didn't go to Church during this time, only to the odd wedding, baptism or Christingle service. I did feel at peace when I was in a church, but didn't take the opportunity to pray and say sorry to God for being too busy for Him. Holding down three jobs couldn't continue. I was so tired that I would lie in bed and cry. I was also unhappy in my marriage. My husband didn't change as I had hoped.

Then an opportunity came to work one job, full time in a large retail store. The job advertised was for a "stockroom keeper", dealing with the stock before it went to the shop floor. I applied and got an interview, not believing for one minute that I was good enough to get it (here we go again). But I was wrong, I did get the job and found the work easy and satisfying. I was learning new skills and worked with an okay group of women with one exception – the manager. I have no excuses about how or why I was drawn in by this woman. Besides that I wanted to fit in. I wanted to be liked… I wanted… I wanted…

Spiritualism and psychics entered my life – tarot card readings and the search for "messages" from those who had departed – with my Nan having died now too. I drew the line at the Ouija board; my Mum had used one when I was little and it scared the life out of me.

These were very dark times for me. I was full of self-doubt, confused about who I was or where I was going. I can remember being at work one day and just thinking to myself, "I don't feel anything". I felt empty, with nothing inside – no emotions, not happy, not angry, not sad. Nothing.

It wasn't long after this that I had a strong feeling to go and buy the local weekly paper in my lunch hour, something I had never done. Thankfully, I did. I was drawn to the jobs section. My hands opened the page to a full size advertisement for "support workers" to work in a new house being built for adults with learning disabilities and challenging behaviour. I couldn't get to the phone quick enough to request an application form. I didn't tell anyone what I was doing, not even my husband. I just knew I had been guided to this, and I had to follow it through. I completed the form, the parts for education, qualifications and experience glaringly blank!

I heard back that there was to be an "open" interview day. There were two dates and the one I was invited to was on my day off. I went along, not knowing what to expect, but certain that I should be there.

It was quite a shock to enter a room where there were twenty-nine other applicants, let me tell you. The two ladies who would be running the new project spoke to us all as a group and as individuals throughout the day. There were scenarios to discuss in small groups, and they would join us to hear our views and problem solving skills. Inevitably, there were some people there who had a wealth of experience and weren't afraid to voice it! This left me feeling totally inadequate at times.

God must have read my thoughts though. Just as I was starting to think, "What on earth am I doing here?" one of the interviewers said, "Can I just say to those of you who may be thinking you aren't qualified for this job, experience can be a hindrance. Coming with an open mind is just as important." Thank you, Lord. So, after a very long and tiring day, I went home hugging my secret to myself.

A fortnight later I got a letter asking me to go for an interview with the two project managers. Once again, it fell on my day off. So off I went, trusting that I was being called to this work and it would all be okay. I can't tell you what was asked of me in the interview because it is all a blur. I do remember, however, I was told that from the thirty people at the first interview day, I was one of only two who had been recalled. They had interviewed another thirty the following day too. That made me feel very good.

I received a letter offering me the job, and I replied, accepting. Now was the time to tell the family, hand in my resignation and figure out how I was going to get to work, as it would be thirty miles away. My husband went ballistic, my manager sulked and my in-laws bought me a cheap little car. Sorted!

Now, to be honest, I was a bit concerned about working with adults with challenging behaviour. Violence at home was one thing, but at work too? Then I got a phone call saying there was to be a delay in opening the new house. Would I be interested in working at a house with six young adults with learning and physical disabilities – that's where my having been in a wheelchair myself would help – ten miles nearer to home? Would I? Yes, please.

Six weeks later the house was ready, but as I was settled where I was, I was given the option to stay. God placed me where He wanted me to be. He had work for me to do.

I was very happy. Finally, I had a purpose and was making a difference to these young people's lives in my small way. I had a grin on my face for weeks and I was getting paid a good wage too!

I was offered training and lapped it up. Someone had dropped out of the National Vocational Qualification (NVQ) in Care. Would I like to take their place? You bet. The only mentor available happened to be one of the executives of the trust I was now working for. A smashing Irish man, supportive and easy to talk to. We got together to sort out a work schedule and decided we would meet at his office once a month.

At the time, all this "falling into place" seemed too good to be true. Oh, ye of little faith. In retrospect, I can see God's hand all over it.

God Uses Me

The niggling feeling started after about three months. Should the clients really be spoken to like that? I didn't like the way some of them were being treated. This was a home where six young adults, all under thirty, lived together. None of them had speech and some were severely physically disabled, in wheelchairs.

Due to the rota system I didn't always get to work with the same members of staff. The majority of staff were good, caring people who had the clients best interests at heart, but there were two women who made me feel uneasy. One was another support worker who worked part-time and the other was the manager. Here we go again. At first, it was just the odd comment, look or something I couldn't quite put my finger on. I must admit I had to search myself to make sure I wasn't the one who had a problem with authority – another manager!

As time went on, I was put on the rota with these two women more often. I don't know if they thought they were safe to behave the way they did because I was still fairly new and hadn't worked in this environment before, or whether they were so far down the road with their abuse and attitudes without being challenged that it became the "norm".

They were clever though. Not much was done in front of me, but they openly told me what they had done and laughed about it. One young woman living in the house had hair past her shoulders. It was lovely. I arrived on shift one day to see that her beautiful hair was close cropped to her head. I was shocked and asked what had happened. I was told by the manager that the young woman had pulled the manager's hair while being lifted into bed the night before. She had cut her hair as a punishment.

When I put her to bed that night I told her I was sorry about her hair. She looked at me so intensely, it touched my heart.

There was a time when another young woman was having epileptic seizures and the manager, in her wisdom (she was a trained nurse) stated, "She's faking them for attention." The manager put her in her room and videoed her through the bedroom window – supposedly to prove her point that once on her own, without an "audience", she would stop.

The rest of the staff were now starting to talk to one another about their concerns. Some left, but no one was prepared to tackle these two abusers or report them. The staff was kept away from the Trust's offices; the manager or the other support worker had all the dealings with them. I, of course, was the exception. I was there once a month to meet with my course mentor. Unbeknown to me, one of the support workers who had recently left bumped into my mentor and told him that I was concerned about what was happening at the house. As I was on a day off, I was ironing when the phone rang. I heard that now familiar Irish accent asking, "Do you need to speak to me?"

I took a deep breath and said, "Yes."

During the thirty-minute drive to the offices I went through every scenario in my mind. What if he didn't believe me? What if I made the situation worse for the clients by speaking up? What if they got rid of me? What if, what if…

Before going in, I prayed that God would guide me and put the right words in my mouth. "Please, Lord, let this go right."

I arrived around 10 a.m. and was still there at 7 p.m. Once I started talking, it all poured out: the abuse, the thefts, the misuse of facilities, the boyfriend staying overnight. All of it. I was exhausted and tearful.

I waited as it sunk in. I had rambled on and on, hardly drawing breath. Then, when I finally stopped talking, I looked at the man sitting opposite me and waited. Please, God, let him believe me. Let him know I am telling him the truth. And please, God, let him do something about all this.

After what felt like an eternity, he looked me in the eyes and said, "Okay, I believe you. We're going to deal with this."

Oh, the relief…

Then he asked me if I would repeat it all to the other Trust executives. Having done that, they both left me alone and I had a very welcome cup of coffee. They returned

51

with the Chief Executive and the Head of Personnel, and I repeated my story for a third time. Notes were taken and I was asked if I was willing to make a formal statement and sign it.

"Well I've come this far," I replied.

With that done, I was told that the pair would be suspended that evening with a view to an internal investigation and hearing taking place. I was offered the opportunity to move to another house, which I declined as I hadn't done anything wrong. Besides, I wanted to support the clients and other members of staff during this crisis. The months that followed were tough. Each woman had a hearing, both of which I attended to give evidence. They then both appealed, so another two hearings followed. Thankfully, all the staff backed me up and gave evidence that resulted in them both being dismissed.

That should have been the end of it, but I suffered from nuisance phone calls – people phoning late at night and hanging up without speaking. I was driving home along the motorway after a late shift one night when a large white van pulled alongside me and continually tried to run me into the barrier. I recognised the boyfriend of the dismissed support worker at the wheel. My husband wasn't best pleased either. Rather than being supportive of me standing up for what was right, he was more concerned with the disruption as I was covering more shifts, and continually asked "Why you?"

I continually thought, "Why *not* me?"

The following year, the support worker took her case to an industrial tribunal where I gave evidence again. Her case was thrown out, but not before I sat through three days of hearing lie after lie from both her and her only witness, the manager. Two years later, I was called to give evidence at the Nurses Governing Body in London. The manager didn't appear. In her absence she was found guilty of thirty-five out of thirty-seven offences and was struck off of the Nurses Register.

Time to Move On

I heard about a job going as a support worker with a community housing scheme for adults with learning disabilities through a social worker I met at a training session. Isn't it amazing how God sends people to us as we need them?

I filled in the application form. This time the qualification and training sections weren't blank. The interview went well and the scheme sounded fascinating. I got the job and was to go on to hold my own diary and be responsible for my own timetable in supporting clients who lived with carer families. I had training in many areas and was promoted to unqualified social worker, made assessments, chaired meetings and monitored the private sector of care homes. Not bad for a kid who left school with no qualifications, eh?

I stayed for eight years and learned many valuable lessons. During this time I hit the big four-O. Age has never bothered me, be it mine or other people's. I still have to work out how old my mum is by how old she was when she got married, how long she was married before I came along and add that to my age!

Anyway, here I was at forty and it hit me hard. What had I done with my life so far? What was I going to do with the rest of it? How long was the rest of it going to be? Was half of it gone already, so quickly?

Two months after my birthday, sometime in early June, my husband and I had an argument one evening over a Chinese meal. The following morning, he left for work without saying goodbye. As I stood brushing my hair in the lounge mirror, I looked at my reflection and said out loud, "Right." For the next thirty minutes or so, time seemed to stand still as I packed clothes, shoes, etc. I wasn't thinking; it was like someone else was controlling my movements. I packed my belongings into my car, kissed the dog on her head and told her to be good. As I locked the front door, I felt a peace come over me.

I set off to work. I was collecting three clients and meeting a colleague at a park for the day with her clients and mine. The weather was glorious and we all enjoyed a picnic lunch. Over lunch, I mentioned that I had left my husband that morning. My colleague was surprised to say the least. As we weren't particularly close, she didn't question me but did ask if I had somewhere to stay. "Of course," I said. Then I thought that maybe I could spend the night in the car parked up somewhere.

The afternoon passed with no further mention of my situation, but as we were getting ready to leave, my colleague suddenly said, "I know you have somewhere to go, but why don't you come and have some dinner with us?" Before I knew what was happening, she had thrust a piece of paper into my hand with her address on it and was gone.

After taking my clients home, I looked at the address, not really wanting to go but now feeling a little scared about where I was going to spend the night.

I turned up on her doorstep, only to be greeted with a mug of coffee and instructions to make myself at home while she got the Shepherd's Pie on the go. We chatted whilst she cooked and I played with her young daughter. It turned out she was a single mum who had survived an abusive relationship. Small world!

With her daughter tucked in bed and the washing up done and put away, we sat to have a coffee and a cigarette before I went on my way.

"You haven't got anywhere to go, have you?" she said.

After a moment's silence, I whispered, "No."

"All I can offer you is a sofa, but it's yours for as long as you need it."

I couldn't believe this act of such kindness. As I lay awake on that sofa that night, I thanked God for once again bringing someone that I needed into my life.

I stayed for two weeks. In that time I spoke to my children and husband, found myself a flat and sorted out my finances. It was liberating as I had never lived alone before. I had always been answerable to someone else, be it my parents, my husband or my children. I really enjoyed getting home from work, closing my front door and lying in the bath for as long as I wanted to with no interruptions.

I must admit I struggled with how quickly the housework and ironing got done though.

After a while my husband and I started to talk, first on the phone and then in person. This was like courting again. We talked a lot about everything. Things were going well, and after six months I moved back home. To his credit he never hit me again, but the physical attacks were replaced by verbal abuse. Whoever said, "Sticks and stones may break my bones, but words will never hurt me" was a fool! As mad as it sounds, there were times when I wished he would lash out as the words stayed in my mind and haunted me for years. I can still quote some of them word for word even now, although they don't hurt anymore.

Life jogged along. Our children were grown. Only our eldest son lived at home. But I had left God behind again…

The Brick Wall

It was decided to appoint a team leader at work and they would look at internal promotion first. There were only two candidates: myself, and a woman who had been working with us for a year. I had worked hard over the eight years of service, always gone the extra mile, was loyal and conscientious. This job was mine...

How conceited was I? A valuable lesson, in retrospect, although not at the time. We can't do anything to earn our place in Heaven, so why did I think I should have the right to a job? I didn't get it, and it didn't help when people said it should have been mine. Sometime later, when I got a phone call from the social worker who had told me about this job eight years earlier, I was interested in the post she was offering me – to be team leader at the unit she was managing. I arranged to go and have a look. Although my inner voice said "No" and I actually vomited on my way home, I said I would take the job. I wanted that title!

Well, I got the title and all that went with it – a client group spaced over three units on one large site, a manager who was either holed up in her office or off-site, a staff team who were untrained and belligerent, and thirty clients with severe mental health issues. Oh yes, I got my title all right, and eighty-eight hour weeks because staff would go off sick at the last minute and I couldn't leave the site understaffed.

My days consisted of intervening between grown men who wanted to rip each others' heads off; listening to a paedophile describe how it was his young nephew's fault that he abused him because he wriggled on his lap; supporting a young woman who had recently given birth and had her baby removed from her for its own safety; and being bitten, spat at or punched.

I dreaded hearing the alarm calling for help. I dreaded hearing my name being called, because it was usually to help restrain someone. What the hell had I got myself into? *Hell* being the operative word, because that's what it felt like… Hell. I couldn't admit defeat though. My husband hadn't wanted me to take the job, there were those I was working with who didn't think a woman was up to it – the team leaders in the past had always been men – and of course there was that little matter of my pride! Then I interviewed a chap for a job as a support worker and was happy to offer it to him. He was really good with the clients, always positive and supportive of me. A *breath of fresh air*. To unwind and bond with each other better, he suggested the team go for a drink after shift at the local pub. This quickly developed into a bit of a ritual.

I told my husband what was happening and who was there, both male and female members of staff. He didn't like it and the old accusation of my having an affair raised its ugly head. One particular night I arrived home after a late shift. I had come straight home, too tired to go for a drink with the others. The lounge light was off. I thought my husband must be in bed, but as I switched on the light, I saw him lying on the sofa. The look on his face was terrifying. He leapt up and came close to my face, shouting, swearing and spitting in my face as he accused me of all sorts.

At that moment I felt like I was dealing with one of the clients I had just left and something inside me died. Here I was, standing in my lounge, briefcase in hand, so tired I didn't know how to stand, and this madman was ranting in my face. This man, who was happy to go on the foreign holidays my extra wages paid for. This man, who was able to drink, smoke and run a car because of the wages I brought in. This man, who said he loved me…

The next day after work when the team were going for a drink I went too. And when, at the end of the evening, I was kissed goodnight I didn't turn away.

What happened over the next week I cannot excuse. All I will say is that had I been in my right mind and not so low and vulnerable, it wouldn't have happened. Heading for a complete physical and mental breakdown, I was unfaithful to my husband twice. Inevitably, once the *breath of fresh air* had got what he wanted, I was dumped.

I was in a bad way. I had done the unforgivable. I had broken my marriage vows. I had turned my back on God.

61

I was alone and sinking fast. My husband wanted me to come home. He could forgive me. We could work it out. So I went home.

I had hit the brick wall. I spent a year laying on the sofa, drugged up on prescription medication. I was scared to answer the phone, and the answering machine was on permanently. I would run upstairs and hide if anyone knocked on the door. I was too afraid even to go into the garden. I was unable to function. I was a prisoner in my own home, but that was okay. I just wanted the world and everyone in it to go away and leave me alone.

They did.

Starting to Live Again

Our eldest son couldn't forgive me for what I had done and moved out. At twenty-six, it was time that he had his own place, and it gave us space to recover and rebuild. I don't believe he has ever forgiven me. There was a brief time when we were reunited and I supported him through his own breakdown, but we are now estranged. He's married with two young sons, and I pray that he learns to deal with his anger issues.

Eventually, I was able to leave the house long enough to attend sessions with a counsellor. As long as someone, usually my husband or daughter, came with me and waited, I could cope. Between them and my younger son (when he was home from working away), someone went everywhere with me. I must have driven them mad, continually asking what day and time it was.

I struggled to stand in a queue, couldn't bear for anyone to be behind me, and if we sat in a café I had to sit facing the door so that I could plan my escape route should I need it. Many times a trip out was cut short because I had to get home to safety.

Oh, the fear…

It was crippling and I couldn't even tell you what I was afraid of.

One day my husband saw an advert in the local paper for a women-only gym. I had gained a lot of weight through my sedentary lifestyle and the medication I was on. He suggested I read it and if interested he would ring and see if I could have a trial. It must have been a good day because I agreed to him ringing and an appointment was made for the next day. We went and I did okay. In time I was going to and from the gym on my own. I lost the weight and my confidence was growing.

It had always been a standing joke that my husband had never actually proposed to me. As a surprise for his fiftieth birthday I got him to drive us to a cottage in the Cotswolds. When he walked in our children were waiting. It was here, as we were about to leave on our last day, that he asked me to renew our vows on our thirtieth wedding anniversary the following year.

The year leading up to our renewal was one of the happiest I had known. We were getting on well, we had a lot to look forward to and I was slowly getting better.

The big day arrived and we had a wonderful service in the church where we had originally married. We even managed to get the same hall we had had for the reception. At some point during the evening I was aware that my husband wasn't in the hall. I found him outside, crying. He said he was just overcome with all we had been through and was happy that we were together. He said sorry for all he had put me through over the years and that he would spend the rest of his life making up for it.

Was I happy? I was over the moon. Finally, *finally*, God had answered my prayers and changed him.

A Work in Progress

Three months later I sat at the dining room table, popping all my medication – sleeping tablets and painkillers – out of their packs. I then proceeded to take them all and washed them down with orange squash. I had left letters for the family and made sure I had clean pyjamas on. I then went to bed… to die.

I remember watching Jeremy Kyle on the TV. Then I was in hospital wired up to a heart monitor. It hadn't worked. Why hadn't it worked? My husband was soon to tell me, "If you had taken the tablets with alcohol, it would have worked." Silly me!

I just wanted to go home, so I discharged myself without seeing the on-duty shrink.

What had possessed me to try and take my own life?

Two things: My husband hadn't changed. He continued to question me about what had happened three years earlier. He didn't believe me and was now, in my opinion, an alcoholic. He didn't go a day without drinking whisky. Secondly, I had been diagnosed with arthritis and I was absolutely terrified of ending up in a wheelchair again.

In my despair I sat on the side of the bath, rocking and crying. I called out, "God, please help me. I'll do whatever it takes. Sweet Jesus, help me."

And from that day, He has helped me.

You see, I had always prayed that God would change others, not me. In my arrogance and ignorance, I wanted *others* changed. Now, I was ready to take responsibility for the things I had done wrong and ask for forgiveness. I spoke with God everyday again, as I had when I was a child, and He heard.

How do I know He heard?

Because things started to happen…

Our daughter was to be married at the church where we, and generations of both our families, had wed and been baptised. So we started attending church regularly every Sunday, and after the wedding, my daughter and I kept going. One day during this time I was sitting in A&E at the local hospital with my daughter. Just a few seats away from us sat a woman with both her wrists bandaged and obviously distressed. When my name was called I went up to her and, touching her arm, said, "I don't know what troubles you, but know that Jesus loves you."

She looked up, smiled and said, "Thank you."

Thank you, Jesus, for letting me show your face to others.

Within three months of being married, my daughter was blessed with a pregnancy. We both decided to attend confirmation preparation classes and were confirmed by the Bishop together while she carried my grandchild. God sent me another blessing during that service. The Bishop was talking about being good enough, and he looked straight at me as he said, "You are good enough."

My husband was continuing to drink heavily and was, by this time, sleeping in a separate bedroom and hiding the bottles. We kept out of each other's way. He took advice from a solicitor as to how we could divorce without leaving the house. I asked him if he was seeing someone, but he wouldn't confirm or deny it.

Soon after, he told me he was moving out and going to live with our eldest son and his wife. He moved out in October and I spent more and more time in prayer and in church. The Vicar's wife ran a women's prayer and praise group which she asked me to go along to. I was only too pleased to be among Christian women, and I enjoyed their fellowship and support. We had Bible study sessions and went to hear Christian speakers.

When my daughter was eight months pregnant, she saw her dad walking in town holding hands with a woman. It turned out my husband *had* been unfaithful to me – my instinct had been right. It was a continuing relationship and, in fact, he is still with her today!

Boy, was I angry. After all the allegations he had made against me, and even though I had done wrong, I had been honest in telling him.

What I didn't appreciate at the time was that God was in the process of clearing the way for what He had planned for me.

I started divorce proceedings.

So to Work

I was in church one Sunday morning with my daughter. We were singing one of my favourite hymns, *How Great Thou Art*, when the tears started to stream down my face. The next thing I knew, I was on the pew. I felt as though I had been hit so hard on the top of my head that it was as if a bolt of heat had gone right through my body and had come out of my feet. I felt as if I had been poleaxed. I was shaking and had to hold on to my daughter for support.

This was the start of my healing process.

I heard God say to me, "Whatever I ask of you, simply say *yes*."

So, when the Vicar asked me to do a reading, I said, "Yes." I couldn't believe how calm I felt. I really enjoyed speaking God's word.

This soon became a regular thing. I was then asked to lead prayers as well. I did, and loved that too.

In March, a month before my fiftieth birthday, the joy of my life came into the world – my grandson, Harry. The first thing I did when I heard he had been born safely was to fall on my knees and thank God.

Oh, the excitement when I first held him in my arms. We looked into each other's eyes, and I felt overwhelming love for this precious gift from God. My continual prayer at this time was, "I'm your servant, Lord. Use me as you will."

The church embraced Harry and everyone welcomed him at his baptism. I was so happy that I thought I would burst. One Sunday one of the readers asked me if I had ever thought about training to be a reader myself.

"No, I don't think so," I said.

"Think about it," he said.

Had I forgotten what God had said to me already? "Simply say *yes*."

Two other people, on separate occasions, asked me the same question. God obviously wanted me to listen. I made an appointment to discuss it with the reader who had originally suggested that I train. We were in an interregnum (without a vicar) at the time. He told me what the training consisted of and that he would approach his old mentor if I was interested.

I *was* interested, but a big concern was how I would be able to finance this training.

"Don't worry about that," was the answer.

So I didn't. I trusted, and before I knew it, a rollercoaster of events took place. I just went with the ride and kept saying, "Yes."

Now, this is how God works – in His time and when He knows we are open to receive His will.

I was originally asked when the vicar of thirty years was still in post. He was a lovely man, but with set beliefs – one being that he didn't agree with women in ministry. If I had approached him to sign the forms I needed to apply for assessment to see if I was suitable to go forward for training, it was most likely he would decline. However, during the interregnum, the Rural Dean (a woman) was overseeing our church. She came to see me, and after an afternoon of discussion she agreed to put me forward.

I attended the first of two "taster" days to see if I felt called to any particular area of ministry – evangelist, pastoral assistant or lay reader. That first Saturday session consisted of a lively bunch of like-minded people, and I knew I wanted to be a part of this community. What truly convinced me that I was in the right place though was yet another confirmation from God. One of the most painful put-downs my husband ever said to me was, "You're nothing special." Up until that day it still hurt. At the end of that first day, everyone was given a folder of information. On a blue sheet (which I still have) was a poem. It's title…? *You're Special.*

The next Saturday session went well and I was getting to accept that God wanted me to commit to this training. The next step was to apply for an interview. I filled in the application and waited. I was called to be interviewed by six people to assess my suitability and to test my "calling". I also had to take part in a debate with other candidates on a subject the interviewers gave us while being observed. Then there was the reading that had to last for a certain length of time to gauge voice projection. I also had to discuss on a one-to-one basis a Christian book I had read recently. It was a very long day and I drove home exhausted.

I had been told that I would hear that evening if I had been successful. I had been home for about fifteen minutes when the phone rang. It was the reader from church asking how I had got on. I filled him in and then said I should hear that night if I had been successful. He said he'd get off the phone to free up the line. I then proceeded to watch the clock as it slowly ticked away the hours.

At nine-thirty, it rang. It was the Warden of Readers. She apologised for the lateness of the hour. *Just tell me.* She'd had a lot of ringing around to do. *JUST tell me.* She asked me how I had felt the day had gone. *JUST TELL me.* She said they had all been very impressed with the candidates. *JUST TELL ME.*

"We are happy to recommend you for reader training."

"Really?"

"Yes, really."

"Are you sure?"

There was laughter at the end of the line. "You'll get a letter of confirmation offering you a place. Well done!" and she was gone.

I was left sitting on the side of my bed, phone still in hand, with tears streaming down my face. This is real, I thought. I phoned my children, my mum and my reader friend. Wow, I was *good enough*.

There was just one more hurdle to get over – the proposal for my being trained had to go before the Parochial Church Council (PCC). Usually, the PCC or the individual would pay for the training or part and part. We were in a situation where neither could afford to pay. Then God stepped in again. My reader friend and his wife offered to sponsor me and pay for my training and my robes. Praise the Lord for their faith in me.

Reaping What We Sow

Whenever I was shopping with my daughter in the town where she lived, we would see a man sitting on the ground outside a well-known frozen food store. I was waiting for my daughter to come out of a shop and took the opportunity to observe him. He just sat there with his dog. He didn't ask for anything and people walked past as if he didn't exist.

My heart went out to him. How awful it is to be invisible. When my daughter came out, I asked her to get a hot drink while I went and bought a packet of sandwiches and a cake. I took them over to the chap on the ground and asked if he would accept something to eat and drink. He agreed, thanked me, and as we walked away, he started to share the sandwiches with his dog. Over the next few weeks, whenever I saw him I would do the same and we would chat for a while. He told me he was homeless but that this hadn't always been the case. He really wanted me to know that this hadn't always been his way of life.

There but for the Grace of God, go I.

Anyway, one day he wasn't there and I didn't see him for a while. I prayed for him every day and asked God to keep him safe. Then soon after, I happened to look out of my lounge window, and who was walking along the path over the road...? My gentleman. He looked clean and was walking with his head up. I never saw him again, but this felt like God letting me know He had heard my prayers.

I haven't told you this story to "big" myself up or to say, "aren't I good?" No, I have told you about it because I believe that we need to show the face of Jesus to those in need. Jesus wouldn't have ignored that dear man sitting on the ground, I'm sure. If only we were more compassionate. That man had a story. He was down on his luck. I wouldn't give him money, as that could have been abused on alcohol or drugs. The price of what I gave him to eat and drink was minimal, but it made such a difference to that individual. He was acknowledged. He was validated.

<u>Matthew 25:35-40</u>

For I was hungry and you gave me something to eat, I was thirsty and you gave me something to drink, I was a stranger and you invited me in, I needed clothes and you clothed me, I was sick and you looked after me, I was in prison and you came to visit me.

"Then the righteous will answer him. 'Lord, when did we see you hungry and feed you or thirsty and give you something to drink? When did we

see you, a stranger, and invite you in, or needing
clothes and clothe you? When did we see you sick
or in prison and go to visit you?'"

"The King will reply, 'Truly I tell you, whatever
you did for one of the least of these brothers and
sisters of mine, you did for me.'"

Backtracking again, the time came when the marital
home had to be sold. There wasn't going to be much
left after the sale, as it had been re-mortgaged and the
property market had dipped. I wasn't up to dealing with
the sale, so my son made all the arrangements and the
estate agents did the viewings. All my memories were tied
up in that house, and I just couldn't show people around
my home. I had to find somewhere to live. Buying a
property wasn't an option, and I really needed somewhere
without steps or stairs. The rheumatoid arthritis had got
progressively worse and my mobility was compromised so
I was registered as disabled. A ground floor flat would be
ideal. I registered with the local council and was informed
I was eligible for a one bedroom flat, which I would be
able to bid for on the internet. So I did as much as I could
and left the rest to God.

I was having a much-needed week away in Devon
with my family when one day my mobile rang. It was a
housing officer asking if I would be interested in a flat.
I said I would, explained I was away and said I would be in
touch when I got back. Later, when I tried to log on to my
bidding account, it wouldn't give me access. I phoned the
council to tell them I couldn't log on.

"You've been allocated a property," I was told. "You aren't eligible to bid on any other properties."

"Oh, could you get someone to phone me with the details, as I only said I would be interested in a flat."

The next day I got a call from a manager at a housing association. He told me where the flat was and the rest of the details. We arranged for me and my son to meet him there the following morning. We arrived a bit early so that we could have a look around. I couldn't believe what I was seeing. Surely this lovely place couldn't be for me. It was a ground floor new build in a block of six flats. Set in the country, it was a walk away from a very pretty village.

The housing manager arrived and showed us into the large one bedroom flat. It had wide doors for wheelchair use (who knows if I will need one in the future) and it was brand spanking new! No one had lived in it before. It would be a great place for my new start. Joy of joys, I could take my beloved golden retriever with me. She has been my constant companion for the past five years. A gift from my daughter and son.

Okay, this was all wonderful but what about the rent? The manager stood at the kitchen work surface, tapping on his calculator, while I glanced anxiously at my son. Please, Lord, if this is where you want me to be, I would be so happy to live here. I could have wept when he gave me the monthly rent payments. It was affordable. I could live here. I could know peace here.

"What happens now, then?" I asked.

"If you're happy, sign here and I'll give you the keys."

Wow – ain't God great!

So, I moved. The house eventually sold, and with the money I got from the sale I was able to furnish my new home.

Yet again, Praise the Lord.

God Looks After My Family Too

There have been three occasions during my grandson's short life (he's now four) that God has intervened and saved him from serious harm and injury.

We were having a day at the seaside and went into a café for some lunch. For some reason I can't explain, as I had never done it before, I sat down on the inside of the table and Harry sat next to me on the outside. Without any warning, he decided to take off. He ran out of the door and straight into the road. My daughter and I shouted and got to our feet as quickly as we could. She made it outside ahead of me to see a large white van heading straight for Harry. He stood in the road, frozen. We both screamed just as the van stopped, inches from where my grandson stood. My daughter ran into the road, grabbed her son and broke down in tears of relief that he hadn't been harmed. I repeatedly said, "Thank you, God, thank you."

I was concerned for the driver of the van. He must be shaken, I thought. He got out of the van, his face ashen.

As I went up to him, he started to shake his head. I asked him if he was alright and he looked at me with a really strange expression on his face.

I repeated my question, gently touching his arm.

I don't know quite what I was expecting him to say, but he said, "I didn't see him, love. I didn't see him. My engine just stopped. The van just *stopped*."

And he was right. There was no sound from the engine. After a few minutes, he got back in to the van, still shaking his head.

People had gathered on the path and were talking to my daughter, saying how lucky the little boy had been. The van had been travelling at a very high speed. They didn't know how it had missed him.

But I knew God's hand had stopped that vehicle and my grandson was saved from serious injury or worse. *Thank you, Lord.*

Another time, my daughter and son-in-law were in their lounge with Harry. My son-in-law had just put a freshly made mug of coffee on the mantelpiece when Harry shot into the chair, reached up and tipped the entire contents of the boiling hot liquid into his lap. Yes, my daughter reacted quickly, removing his clothing and getting him under cool water, while an ambulance was summoned. When the paramedics and doctor arrived, they couldn't believe that he wasn't marked at all! I could. Once again, my sweet Lord had saved him from injury.

On the third occasion he fell from the top of a fireman's pole climbing frame, straight onto his back. He was badly winded and didn't move for a while. An ambulance was called as he could have had spinal or internal injuries. Every precaution was taken to keep him still and stable. Yet again, the medical professionals were amazed. There wasn't a mark on him, not even a bruise.

Harry loves being in church and is always asking me about what I have been doing. One day we were having Sunday lunch together and talking about church. I asked him if he wanted to be a vicar when he grows up. He thought for a while before saying, "No, thank you. I don't want a white beard."

I had a good laugh at that one. He is so funny and loving. I pray that he will grow up knowing Jesus as his Saviour and Lord.

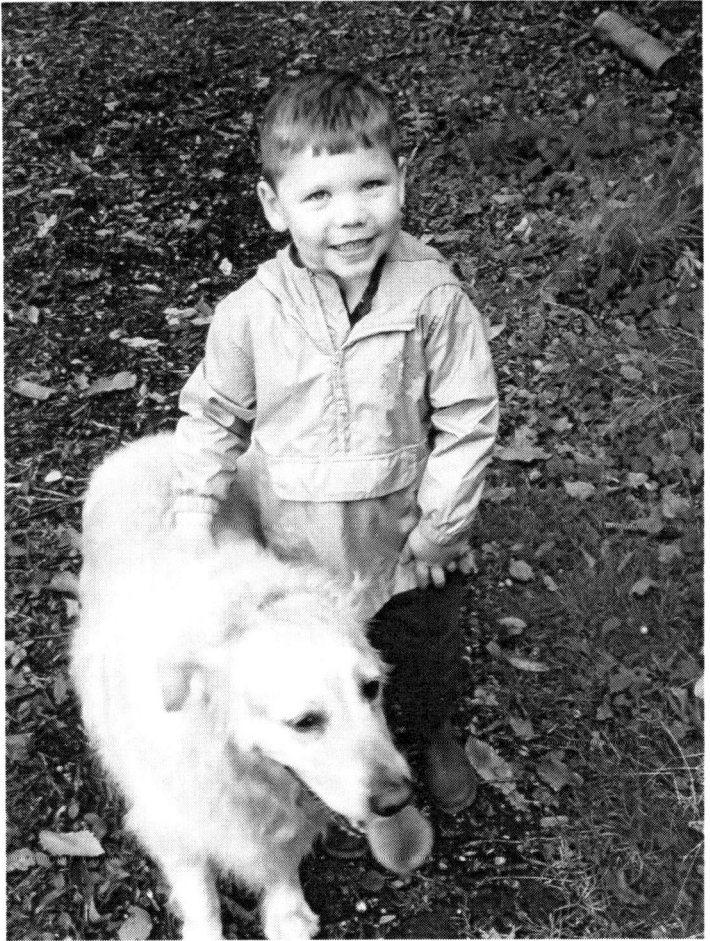
My joy! Bridie and grandson Harry

Training to be a Lay Reader

I am now in my third and last year of training. I have passed the Ministerial Theology course and have been accredited by the University. Yes, I said *the University*! On the bottom of the certificate it says: *This certificate enables access to the second level of study for a Bachelors degree*. I laughed out loud when I read that. Little old me achieving so much. Who'd have thought it?

I can't see myself taking up that option but, hey, as my dear friend – the reader who helped me train and is now working towards becoming a vicar – says, "Never say never."

The past two years have been hard work, but so rewarding. I have learned so much. My values and beliefs have been challenged. I have learned to read the Bible in a mature way, and I have learned to be still and listen to that quiet voice inside. The tutors have been a wealth of knowledge. Everyone on the course has had their own story and it has been a privilege to share with them. I have made some friends for life. We have laughed together and cried together. We've supported each other, encouraged and kept each other going when we wanted to give up. It's been one heck of a journey and it's not over yet. We still have this year to complete but it isn't as demanding as the past two years have been with assignments and deadlines to meet.

I am so blessed with the ministry team I work with at church too. The new vicar was appointed and has been supportive of my ministry from day one. My reader friend left earlier this year, and as I said, he is now training for ordination. The other reader is a great support. He has been at the church for over thirty years and is a wealth of information. I preach, lead services, take a women's fellowship, am a church warden and when I have had the training, I hope to be able to officiate at funerals.

Talking of funerals, I participated in the funeral of a dear friend only last week. The vicar, the reader and I took part and it was such a privilege. You know how in life there are those people who's opinions really matter to you? Well, this lady was one of those. I had known her for about six years and she was one of the ladies who met each week with the old vicar's wife. I had warmed to her straight away. Physically, she reminded me of my own dear nan with her white hair, sparkling eyes and ready smile. When I first started going to the group, I was a bit of a mess. There were lots of tears and I was in need of support. She was so kind to me. She encouraged me to pray and to take my sorrow to God. Not everyone was in support of my going forward to be trained for ministry. There were still those women who believed that only men should be at the front; she wasn't one of them and offered me support and encouragement from the start.

When she was ill and unable to get to Church, I would take communion to her and we would pray together. When she was well enough, the group of ladies would meet at her house and we would talk and sing. One of her favourite worship songs was *In Christ Alone* and the last verse has come to be a witness statement for me.

> *No guilt in life, no fear in death,*
> *This is the power of Christ in me;*
> *From life's first cry to final breath,*
> *Jesus commands my destiny.*
> *No power of hell, no scheme of man,*
> *Can ever pluck me from His hand;*
> *Till He returns or calls me home,*
> *Here in the power of Christ I'll stand!*[1]

When her funeral arrangements were being made, I went along to meet with her son as well. We had met a couple of times before but only to say *hello*. During the arrangements he told us about a poem that he had written and that he would like me to read at the funeral. I asked if he had a copy for me to practice from. It was then that he told us he had written a book, guided by God. At our next visit I was given a copy as a gift. That night I started reading it and didn't stop until I had finished it.

Two days later, I was at my laptop writing this…

1 Stuart Townsend & Keith Getty – Copyright 2001, Thankyou Music

Some Thoughts

The last thing I would want you to think is that I am some sort of "do-gooder-Christian-know-it-all". You couldn't be further from the truth. I'm human and I mess up. The difference is I'm quick to realise it and to say sorry to God. I'm so much stronger and more confident than I used to be. That comes from knowing that I'm loved, and that I'm special to God. I'm His child.

I love to laugh – it's such a good medicine! You know, there are people who call themselves Christians… some who think all they have to do is turn up on Sunday for an hour service. Others say, you don't have to go to church to be a Christian. I disagree. God made us to live in fellowship together. We need to study the Bible, pray, support one another and share the joys and troubles of this life with one another.

The main commandment is: *Love one another, as I have loved you.*

And how did Jesus love us? He loved us with compassion,

humility and kindness, but He also rebuked and corrected those who needed it.

In the past, I have smoked and drunk too much. At the time I used them both as crutches. But I don't need them now. I am happy and at peace, and I really want others to have that. I still have health issues and problems, but that's life. God never promised it would be easy, but He did promise *to be with you, even until the end of days.*

Over the past couple of years, there has been a worship song that has haunted me. We'd sing it in church. It would play on the CD player in a friend's car. Visiting a Christian bookshop, it would be playing in the background. It pops into my head as I'm washing up or making the bed, and before I know it, I'm singing aloud.

The chorus goes like this:

> *Here I am Lord,*
> *Is it I, Lord?*
> *I have heard You calling in the night.*
> *I will go, Lord,*
> *If you lead me;*
> *I will hold Your people in my heart.*[1]

God speaks to me all the time. He gives me what He wants me to preach about – usually in a dream– and then I will get confirmation two or three other ways. One of the most memorable was for this year's Mothering Sunday service. I dreamt that I was to speak about hands. The next day an old country song came on the radio that hadn't been

1 Daniel L. Schuttle – Copyright 1981, Daniel L Schumm & New Dawn Music

played by the DJ before. It was called *My Grandmother's Hands*. Two days later I walked into a church where we were doing some training and there was there was a display of praying hands!

Okay, Lord, I got it – *hands*.

I didn't write anything for the sermon. I just gave it over to God, and the Holy Spirit spoke through me about what our hands do in a lifetime and what Jesus' hands did for us. The feedback I got from the congregation was so positive, and I know that hearts were touched that day. I pray that God will continue to use me in this way.

If you are seeking, lonely, sad or confused, try Jesus. What have you got to lose? I've told you what you can gain. Don't be misled – I'm not talking about "religion" here. Religion gets in the way all the time. You know when scientists talk about the Big Bang Theory and how the world came to be? Well, maybe it did happen that way but instead at God's hand, at His voice. The images of the universe seen through the Hubble telescope are truly amazing. God did that too.

However, we don't have to go into outer space to see the amazing world God has made. Just look at the trees in autumn as the leaves change colour: greens, oranges, yellows, reds. Look at a rainbow. The other day we had some strange weather here – sunshine and showers, one after another all morning. The sky was full of rainbows… amazing.

Then, of course, there is the miracle of birth. Yes, scientists have found out about DNA, etc., but God has used people to learn and share things about Him and

His world throughout all time. While I'm on a roll here, another thing I want to mention is if Darwin's Theory of Evolution is correct and the human race is descended from apes, why are the apes still around? Surely if something evolves, the "old" dies out?

Anyway, I'll leave that thought with you.

I don't know why God wants me to write this book, I only know that He does.

I wonder if it is to give those who may read it the promise of hope and the knowledge that all things are possible with Him. I don't know at this point if it will ever be published… I can only trust that it will. He has sent the right people to me as I have needed them, so I will wait on Him.

If you do get to read it, I send you love and blessings, always.

Leigh

Lightning Source UK Ltd.
Milton Keynes UK
UKOW050601310712

196816UK00001B/8/P

9 781781 320495